D0231599

SCOTLAND

LET'S GET QUIZZICAL

GWION PRYDDERCH

SCOTLAND: LET'S GET QUIZZICAL
COPYRIGHT © GWION PRYDDERCH, 2014
ALL RIGHTS RESERVED.

NO PART OF THIS BOOK MAY BE REPRODUCED BY ANY MEANS, NOR TRANSMITTED, NOR
TRANSLATED INTO A MACHINE LANGUAGE, WITHOUT THE WRITTEN
PERMISSION OF THE PUBLISHERS.

GWION PRYDDERCH HAS ASSERTED HIS RIGHT TO BE IDENTIFIED AS THE AUTHOR OF THIS WORK IN
ACCORDANCE WITH SECTIONS 77 AND 78 OF THE COPYRIGHT,
DESIGNS AND PATENTS ACT 1988.

CONDITION OF SALE
THIS BOOK IS SOLD SUBJECT TO THE CONDITION THAT IT SHALL NOT, BY WAY OF TRADE OR
OTHERWISE, BE LENT, RE-SOLD, HIRED OUT OR OTHERWISE CIRCULATED IN ANY FORM OF
BINDING OR COVER OTHER THAN THAT IN WHICH IT IS PUBLISHED AND WITHOUT A SIMILAR
CONDITION INCLUDING THIS CONDITION BEING IMPOSED ON THE SUBSEQUENT PURCHASER.

SUMMERSDALE PUBLISHERS LTD
46 WEST STREET
CHICHESTER
WEST SUSSEX
PO19 1RP
UK

WWW.SUMMERSDALE.COM
PRINTED AND BOUND IN CHINA
ISBN: 978-1-84953-596-0

SUBSTANTIAL DISCOUNTS ON BULK QUANTITIES OF SUMMERSDALE BOOKS
ARE AVAILABLE TO CORPORATIONS, PROFESSIONAL ASSOCIATIONS AND OTHER
ORGANISATIONS. FOR DETAILS CONTACT NICKY DOUGLAS BY TELEPHONE:
+44 (0) 1243 756902, FAX: +44 (0) 1243 786300 OR EMAIL: NICKY@SUMMERSDALE.COM

THIS PAIR ONLY APPEARS ONCE ON THE OPPOSITE PAGE

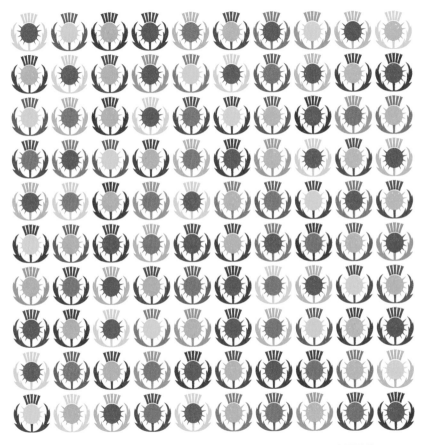

WHAT HEIGHT MUST A SCOTTISH MOUNTAIN EXCEED TO BE CLASSED AS A 'MUNRO'?

A) 1,000 FT

B) 3,000 FT

C) 5,000 FT

EDINBURGH

GLASGOW

DUNDEE

PERTH

ABERDEEN

INVERNESS

STIRLING

```
D S G E E N G O W N
E S L A B E S P E H
D E A U I D S E G A
I N S F G A D R N M
N R G A L R U T I N
E E O G E B N H L B
E V W B N I D N R S
N N A I K N E U I O
B I D J S V E D T I
A E S T I P E R S G
```

THE WORD 'WHISKY' IN THE NATIVE GAELIC TONGUE IS *UISGE BEATHA*, BUT WHAT IS ITS LITERAL TRANSLATION?

A) WATER OF LIFE

B) ELIXIR OF DEATH

C) LIQUID HAPPINESS

SPOT THE DIFFERENCE – THERE'S ONLY ONE!

THIS PAIR ONLY APPEARS ONCE ON THE OPPOSITE PAGE

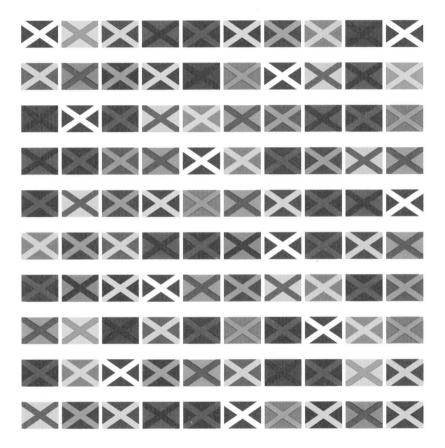

YOU'RE 12–8 DOWN IN THE CALCUTTA CUP – YOU NEED A TRY!

WHAT IS THE CLYDE AUDITORIUM IN GLASGOW COMMONLY KNOW AS?

A) THE CROISSANT

B) SYDNEY TWO

C) THE ARMADILLO

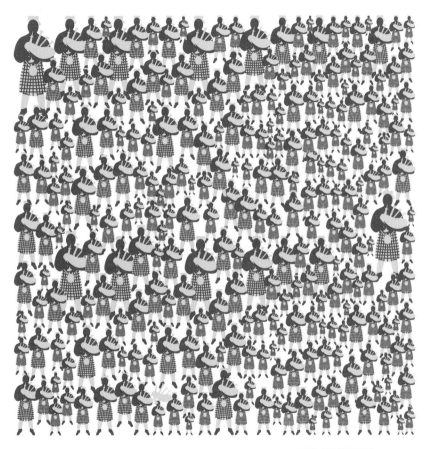

THIS PAIR ONLY APPEARS ONCE ON THE OPPOSITE PAGE

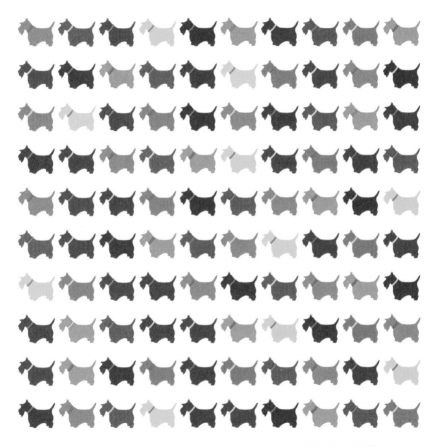

THE TRADITIONAL FOLK SONG 'AULD LANG SYNE' IS BASED ON A POEM BY SCOTTISH LEGEND ROBERT BURNS. WHAT DOES THE TITLE REFER TO?

A) AN OLD WOMAN NAMED LANG SYNE

B) THE 'OLDEN DAYS'

C) BROTHERLY LOVE

GET THE GOLDEN EAGLE BACK TO THE NEST WITH THE HUNGRY CHICKS!

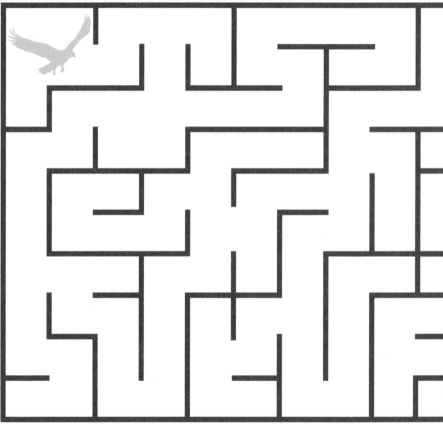

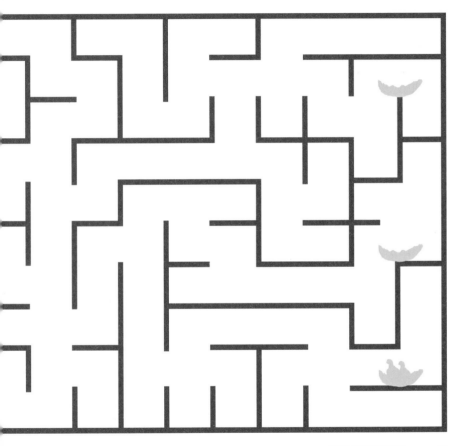

FIND AND CLIMB 'BEN NEVIS'

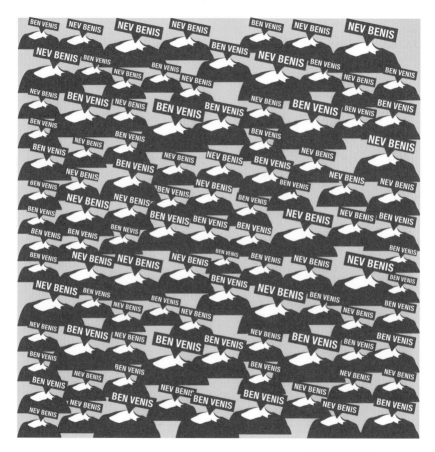

NEW SLAINS CASTLE IN ABERDEEN IS SAID TO HAVE INSPIRED A CERTAIN VICTORIAN AUTHOR, BUT WHICH ONE?

A) ROBERT LOUIS STEVENSON

B) BRAM STOKER

C) MARY SHELLEY

SPOT THE DIFFERENCE – THERE'S ONLY ONE!

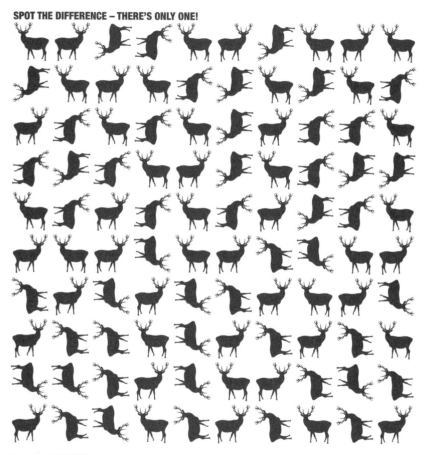

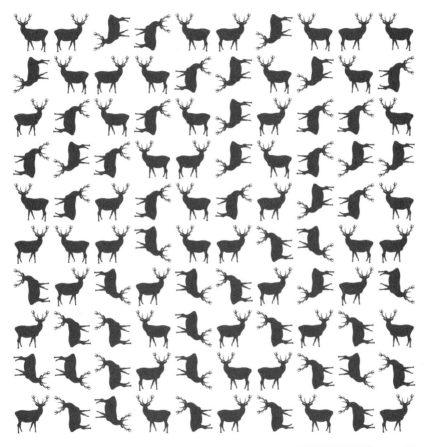

WHICH OF THE FOLLOWING SCOTTISH ISLANDS IS FAMOUS FOR PROVIDING THE GRANITE USED TO MAKE CURLING STONES?

A) AILSA CRAIG

B) SKYE

C) JURA

HIS
MAJESTY'S

SCOTLAND IS KNOWN FOR ITS DELICIOUS SALMON. HOW HIGH CAN AN ATLANTIC SALMON JUMP?

A) 3 FT

B) 7 FT

C) 11 FT

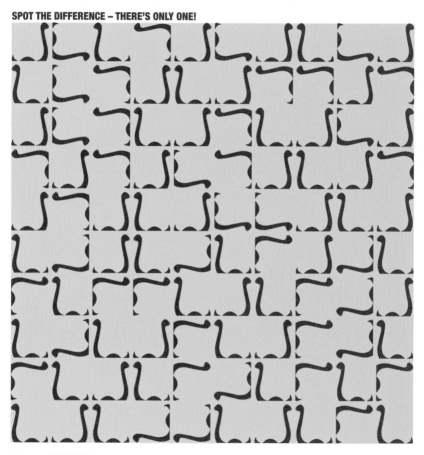

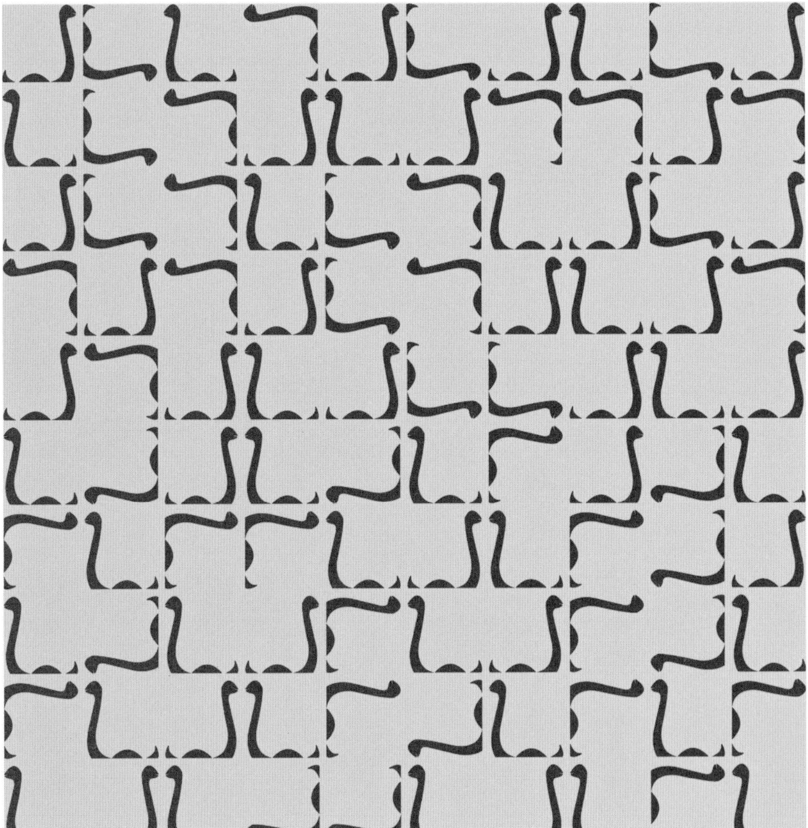

THIS PAIR ONLY APPEARS ONCE
ON THE OPPOSITE PAGE

 **FIND THE THISTLE**

ADDRESS TO A HAGGIS

FAIR FA' YOUR HONEST, SONSIE FACE,
GREAT CHIEFTAIN O' THE PUDDIN-RACE!
ABOON THEM A' YE TAK YOUR PLACE,
PAINCH, TRIPE, OR THAIRM
WEEL ARE YE WORDY O' A GRACE
AS LANG'S MY ARM.

INTESTINE

WORTHY

ABOVE

CHEERFUL

STOMACH

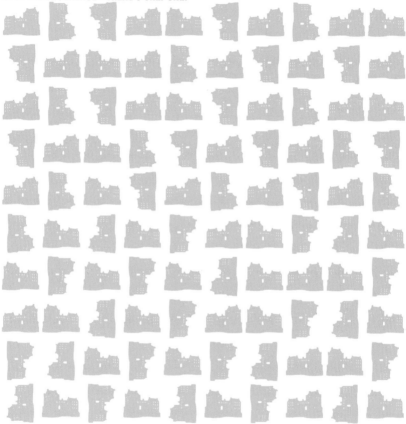

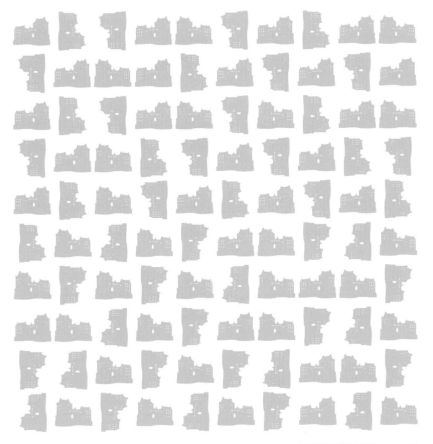

SCOTTY'S GETTING WET, GET HIM BACK TO HIS KENNEL!

SCOTTY

CONNERY (SEAN)
LENNOX (ANNIE)
MCGREGOR (EWAN)
BUTLER (GERARD)
MACDONALD (KELLY)
FERGUSON (ALEX)
MURRAY (ANDY)
BOYLE (SUSAN)
TUNSTALL (KT)
RAMSAY (GORDON)

A	B	M	C	G	R	E	G	O	R
F	U	B	B	C	A	D	E	X	M
E	T	M	O	L	M	K	H	F	A
R	L	N	Y	O	S	P	R	T	C
G	E	S	L	X	A	B	M	N	D
U	R	H	E	D	Y	O	U	N	O
S	G	I	N	W	O	X	R	M	N
O	N	C	O	N	N	E	R	Y	A
N	N	T	U	N	S	T	A	L	L
O	L	E	N	N	O	X	Y	W	D

IN 1933, NESSIE FOOTPRINTS WERE FOUND ON THE SHORES OF LOCH NESS. THE BRITISH MUSEUM LATER PROVED THEM TO BE FAKE, BUT WHAT WERE THEY REALLY MADE BY?

A) A MAN WEARING FLIPPERS

B) A PARTICULARLY LARGE COW

C) A STUFFED HIPPOPOTAMUS FOOT

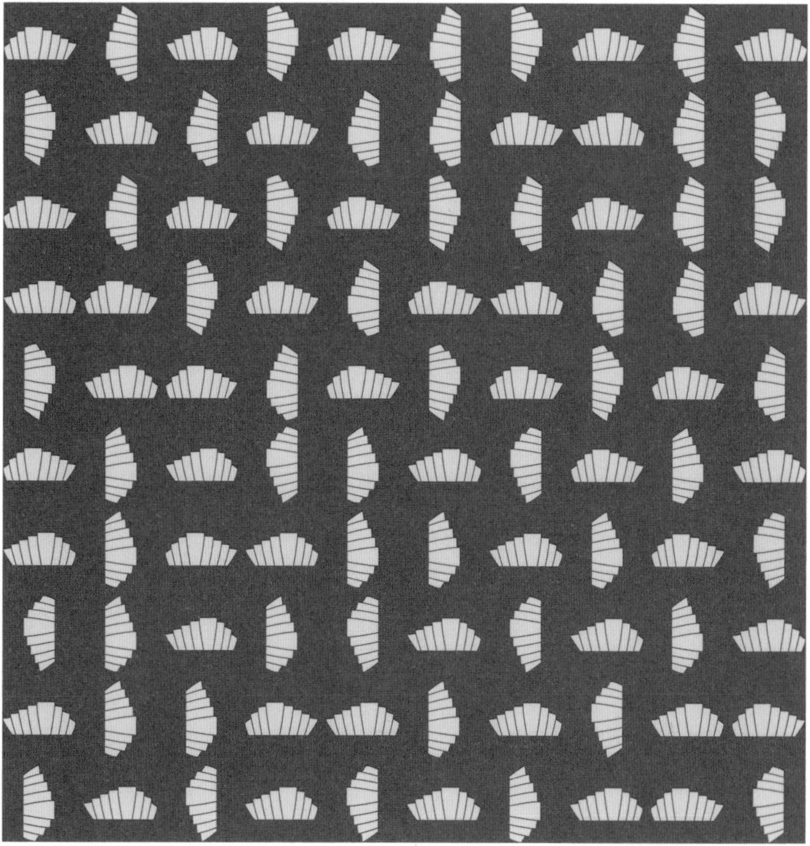

**THIS PAIR ONLY APPEARS ONCE
ON THE OPPOSITE PAGE**

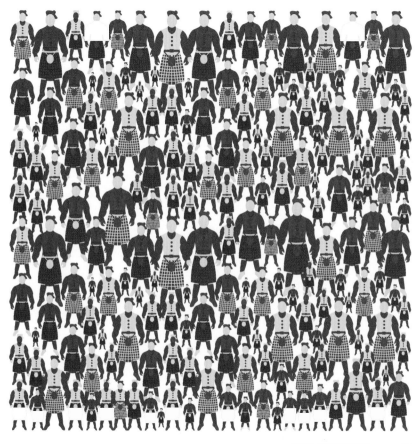

IT'S BURNS NIGHT – GET THE HAGGIS TO YOUR HUNGRY GUESTS!

THE UNIVERSITY OF ST ANDREWS IS SCOTLAND'S OLDEST UNIVERSITY – WHEN WAS IT FOUNDED?

A) 1314

B) 1413

C) 1514

 **FIND THE BLUE HIGHLAND COW**

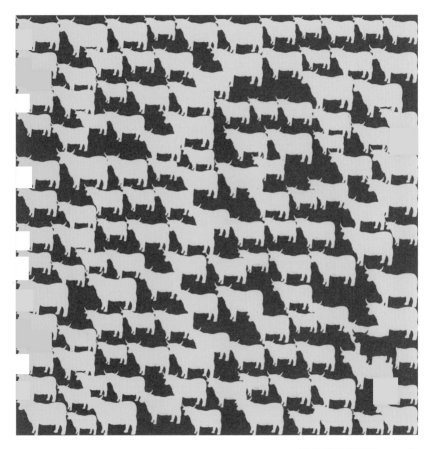

ROWIE A FLAKY, BUTTERY BREAD ROLL

BRIDIE A MEAT PASTRY OR PIE

CRANACHAN CREAM, WHISKY, HONEY, RASPBERRIES AND OATMEAL

FINNAN A 'FINNAN HADDIE' IS A SMOKED HADDOCK

HAGGIS MINCED OFFAL, SUET, ONIONS, OATMEAL, SPICES

BANNOCK A BREAD THE SAME CONSISTENCY AS A SCONE

STOVIES STEWED POTATOES, ONIONS AND LEFTOVER MEAT

TAIBLET A SUGARY CONFECTION MADE WITH CONDENSED MILK

H	N	B	S	C	W	G	G	I	S
S	N	T	F	G	H	J	K	L	S
C	H	A	G	G	I	S	V	S	T
B	R	I	D	I	E	N	N	R	O
A	O	B	A	F	B	C	V	O	V
N	P	L	I	I	U	T	R	P	I
N	K	E	L	N	R	O	W	I	E
O	J	T	H	N	G	F	D	E	S
C	R	A	N	A	C	H	A	N	I
K	M	N	B	N	V	C	A	P	O

WHICH ONE OF THE FOLLOWING IS NOT AN ITEM TRADITIONALLY GIVEN AS A NEW YEAR'S GIFT IN SCOTLAND?

A) A PIECE OF COAL

B) SHORTBREAD

C) A SHINY PENNY

THIS PAIR ONLY APPEARS ONCE
ON THE OPPOSITE PAGE

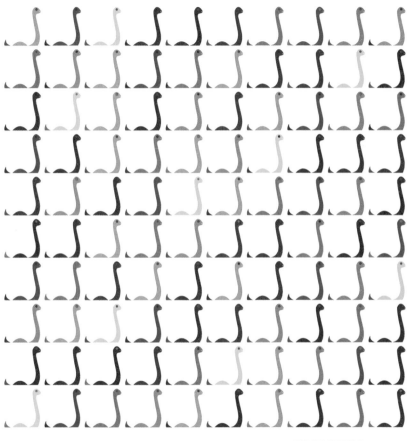

C_____ S_____

L__N__

C_____ N____ P___

G_____ C_____

B____ M_____,K_____

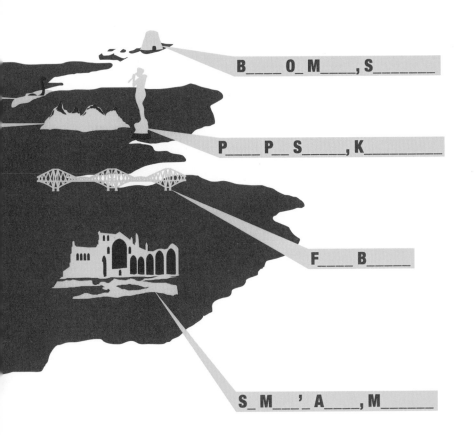

B____ O_M____, S_____

P____ P_S____, K_____

F____ B_____

S_M___'_ A____, M_____

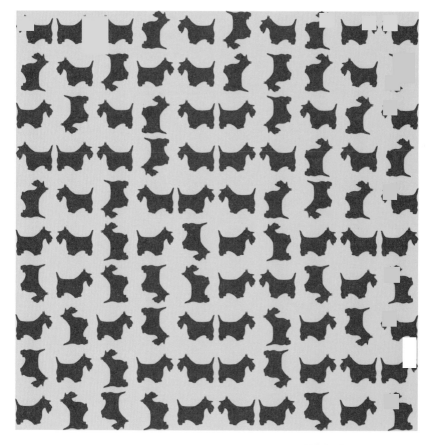

**WHEN THE MAGNIFICENT FORTH RAIL BRIDGE
WAS FIRST REFURBISHED, APPROXIMATELY
HOW MANY LITRES OF PAINT WERE USED?**

A) **160,000**

B) **200,000**

C) **240,000**

THIS PAIR ONLY APPEARS ONCE ON THE OPPOSITE PAGE

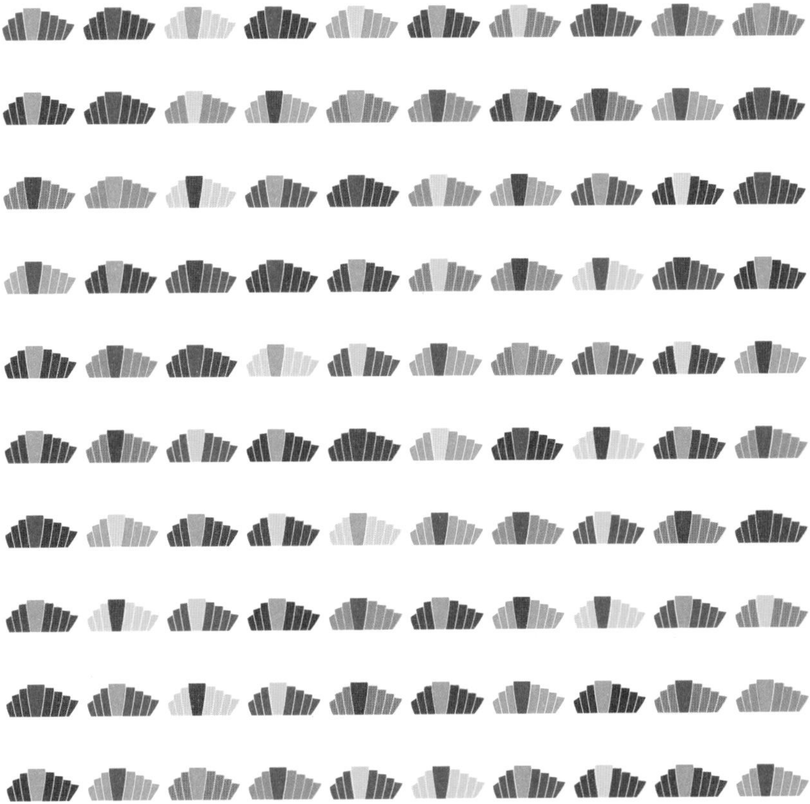

IT'S AD 793 – GET BACK TO YOUR ROUNDHOUSE, THE VIKINGS ARE COMING!

HUNTERS ACROSS SCOTLAND WELCOME THE 'GLORIOUS TWELFTH' (OF AUGUST) AT WHICH TIME THEY ARE PERMITTED TO SHOOT...

A) **RED GROUSE**

B) **RED KITE**

C) **RED-NECKED PHALAROPE**

THE PARADE STARTS IN TWO MINUTES, FIND YOUR GLENGARRY CAP!

THIS PAIR ONLY APPEARS ONCE
ON THE OPPOSITE PAGE

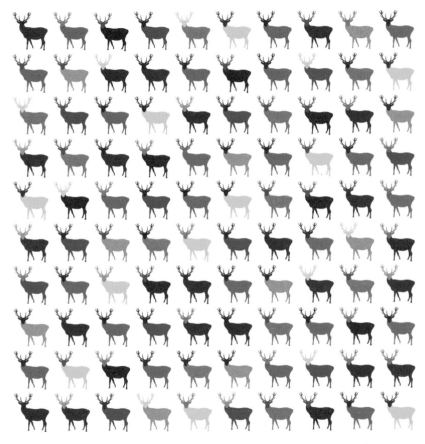

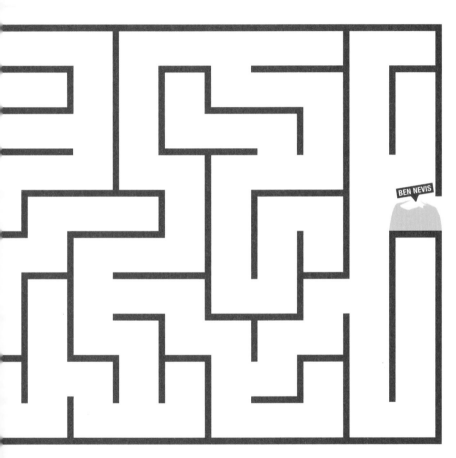

BEN NEVIS

WHICH ONE OF THE FOLLOWING IS NOT AN ITEM OF TRADITIONAL HIGHLAND DRESS?

A) SPORRAN

B) JABOT

C) BAWBEE

SCOTTISH ISLANDS

ARRAN
SKYE
ISLAY
MULL
ST KILDA
BARRA
AILSA CRAIG
BENBECULA
BRESSAY
COLONSAY
STRONSAY

```
W  B  E  N  B  E  C  U  L  A
A  R  R  A  N  R  R  E  T  I
Y  E  U  I  O  P  M  U  L  L
A  S  T  K  I  L  D  A  R  S
I  S  L  A  Y  S  D  F  R  A
G  A  G  H  S  K  Y  E  J  C
K  Y  L  C  V  B  N  M  P  R
T  R  U  W  P  B  A  R  R  A
M  S  T  R  O  N  S  A  Y  I
C  O  L  O  N  S  A  Y  N  G
```

SCOTLAND HAS A NUMBER OF 'UNOFFICIAL' NATIONAL ANTHEMS. WHICH OF THE FOLLOWING SONGS HAS NEVER BEEN USED IN THIS PATRIOTIC CONTEXT?

A) 'FLOWER OF SCOTLAND'

B) 'SCOTS WHA HAE'

C) 'SCOTLAND THE GLORIOUS'

ANSWERS

P4-5

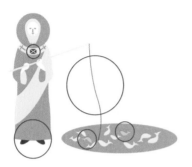

P6-7

P8-9 B) 3,000 FT

P10-11

P12-13 A) WATER OF LIFE

P14-15

P16-17

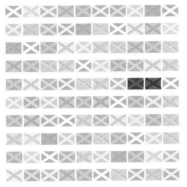

P18-19

P22-23

P24-25

P26-27 B) THE 'OLDEN DAYS'

P28-29

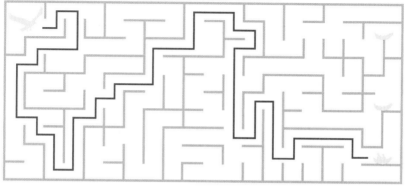

P30-31

P32-33 B) BRAM STOKER

P34-35

P36-37 A) AILSA CRAIG

P38-39

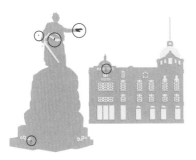

P44-45

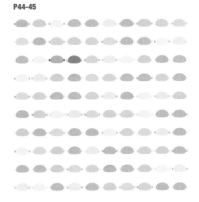

P40-41 C) 11 FT

P42-43

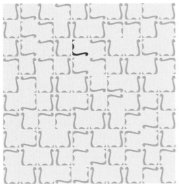

P46-47

P48–49

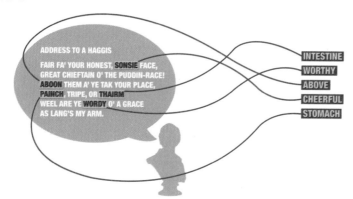

ADDRESS TO A HAGGIS

FAIR FA' YOUR HONEST, SONSIE FACE,
GREAT CHIEFTAIN O' THE PUDDIN-RACE!
ABOON THEM A' YE TAK YOUR PLACE,
PAINCH, TRIPE, OR THAIRM
WEEL ARE YE WORDY O' A GRACE
AS LANG'S MY ARM.

INTESTINE
WORTHY
ABOVE
CHEERFUL
STOMACH

P50–51

P52–53

P54-55

P56-57 C) A STUFFED HIPPOPOTAMUS FOOT

P58-59

P60-61

P62-63

P64-65

P66-67 B) 1413

P68-69

P70-71

P72-73 C) A SHINY PENNY

P74-75

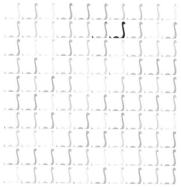

P76-77

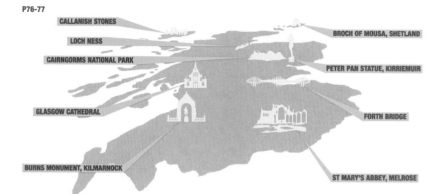

CALLANISH STONES

LOCH NESS

CAIRNGORMS NATIONAL PARK

GLASGOW CATHEDRAL

BURNS MONUMENT, KILMARNOCK

BROCH OF MOUSA, SHETLAND

PETER PAN STATUE, KIRRIEMUIR

FORTH BRIDGE

ST MARY'S ABBEY, MELROSE

P80-81 C) 240,000

P78-79

P82-83

P84-85

P86-87 A) RED GROUSE

P88-89

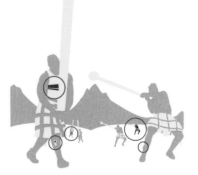

P90-91

P92-93

P94-95

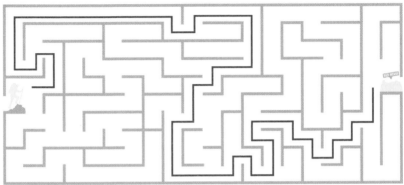

P96-97 C) BAWBEE

P98-99

P100-101 C) 'SCOTLAND THE GLORIOUS'

IF YOU'RE INTERESTED IN FINDING OUT MORE ABOUT OUR BOOKS, FIND US ON FACEBOOK AT SUMMERSDALE PUBLISHERS AND FOLLOW US ON TWITTER AT @SUMMERSDALE.

WWW.SUMMERSDALE.COM